COCKTAILS

Dear Jenny & Ryan

Here's a toast from me to you!
Congratulations on your engagement.
I wish I could be there to buy a drink for you; this book will have to do for now!

Congrats!!

Love,
Jordan

Cocktails

Linda Doeser

BARNES
&NOBLE
BOOKS
NEW YORK

NOTE
Recipes using uncooked eggs should be avoided by infants, the elderly, pregnant women,
convalescents, and anyone suffering from an illness.

Contents

Introduction

Precisely where the word "cocktail" came from is uncertain. A popular piece of folklore describes how a Mexican princess named Xoctl offered a mixed drink to an American visitor to her father's court, and how the visitor then confused her name with that of the drink itself. Modern etymologists mostly agree, however, that the word derives from *coquetel*, a French, wine-based drink.

Whatever the origins of the word cocktail, mixed drinks have existed since ancient times, and the first recognizable cocktail dates from about the sixteenth century. The bourbon-based Old Fashioned first appeared at the end of the eighteenth century, and we know that the word cocktail was already in use in 1809 in the United States.

Popular among the style-conscious and wealthy in the United States, cocktails were served before dinner in the most exclusive houses and hotels until World War I made them unfashionable.

Following the war, young people developed a taste for a new range of cocktails. Ironically, Prohibition in the

United States in the 1920s spurred on their development. Illegally produced liquor often tasted poisonous—and sometimes was—so its flavor needed to be disguised with fruit juices and mixers, which aided the cocktail's development. No doubt, the naughtiness of drinking alcoholic cocktails also added to their appeal to the "bright young things" of the time.

The craze quickly crossed the Atlantic, to where the quality of gin and whiskey was more consistent, and the best hotels in London, Paris, and Monte Carlo soon boasted their very own cocktail bars.

World War II brought an end to such revelry and, although drunk occasionally, cocktails remained out of style for decades until an exuberant renaissance in the 1970s. This resulted in another new generation of recipes and the cocktail has gone in and out of vogue ever since.

Nowadays, with more fruits and drinks available from around the world, the cocktail shaker is once again essential equipment in every fashionable city bar.

Equipment

Classic cocktails are either shaken or stirred. A shaker is an essential and relatively inexpensive piece of equipment, consisting of a container with an inner, perforated lid and an outer lid. Both lids are secured while the mixture is shaken, together with cracked ice, and then the cocktail is strained through the perforated lid into a glass.

A mixing glass is simply a medium-sized pitcher in which stirred cocktails can be mixed. It is usually made of uncolored glass, so that you can see what you are doing.

A long-handled bar spoon is the perfect tool for stirring and a small strainer prevents the ice cubes—used during mixing—finding their way into the cocktail glass. Some modern cocktails, including slushes, are made in a blender or food processor, so if you have one of these in the kitchen, by all means make use of it. Any cocktail that is made by shaking can also be made in a blender.

Measuring cups, sometimes called "jiggers", and spoons are essential for getting the proportions right —guessing does not work. A corkscrew, bottle-opener, and sharp knife are crucial.

Other useful, but non-essential tools include a citrus reamer, an ice bucket and tongs, a punch bowl, a glass serving pitcher, and a zester or grater. If you have a juicer, this is useful for making large quantities of fresh juice for cocktails, and for preparing a hangover cure the morning after!

Glasses

You can serve cocktails in any glasses you like—they are meant to be fun, after all, not an assault course. Small, V-shaped, stemmed glasses, known as cocktail glasses, may be worth buying specially, but it is not essential to have a full range of Old-fashioned, Highball, Collins glasses, and so on. Medium and small straight-sided glasses, and wine glasses cover most contingencies. Since part of their appeal is often visual, cocktails are best served in clear, uncut glass. Try chilling the glasses in the refrigerator beforehand to ensure that your cocktails are served cold.

Techniques

To crack ice, put ice cubes into a strong plastic bag and hit it against an outside wall, or put the ice between clean cloths on a sturdy surface and crush with a wooden mallet or rolling pin. To make crushed ice, use the same method but break the ice into much smaller pieces.

Glasses can be decorated with a sugar frosting—or even fine or coarse salt in the case of the Margarita or Salty Dog. A simple way to do this is to rub the rim of the glass with a wedge of lemon or lime and then dip the rim into a saucer of superfine sugar or fine salt until it is evenly coated.

To make sugar syrup, put
4 tablespoons water and
4 tablespoons superfine sugar
into a small pan and stir over
low heat until the sugar has
dissolved. Bring to a boil, then
continue to boil, without
stirring, for 1–2 minutes. Cool,
then refrigerate in a covered
container for up to 2 weeks.

To make a shaken cocktail, put
cracked ice into a cocktail
shaker and pour over the
other ingredients immediately.
Secure the lids and shake
vigorously for 10–20 seconds,
by which time the outside of
the shaker should be coated
in condensation. Strain into a
glass and serve straight away.

Classic Cocktails

Classic Cocktail

It cannot lay claim to being the first, or even the only classic, but it has all the characteristic hallmarks of sophistication associated with cocktails.

wedge of lemon
1 tsp superfine sugar
4–6 cracked ice cubes
2 measures brandy
½ measure clear Curaçao
½ measure Maraschino
½ measure lemon juice
lemon peel twist, to decorate

serves 1

❶ Rub the rim of a chilled cocktail glass with the lemon wedge and then dip in the sugar to frost.
❷ Put the cracked ice into a cocktail shaker. Pour the brandy, Curaçao, Maraschino, and lemon juice over the ice and shake vigorously until a frost forms.
❸ Strain into the frosted glass and decorate with the lemon twist.

Sangaree

Like Sangria, the name of this cocktail is derived from the Spanish word for blood and it was originally made with wine. Nowadays, it is more usually made with a spirit base, but whatever is used, it is invariably flavored with nutmeg.

6 cracked ice cubes
2 measures brandy
1 measure sugar syrup
(see page 11)
club soda, to top off
1 tsp port
pinch of freshly
grated nutmeg

serves 1

❶ Put the ice cubes into a chilled highball glass. Pour the brandy and sugar syrup over the ice and top off with club soda. Stir gently to mix.
❷ Float the port on top by pouring it gently over the back of a teaspoon and sprinkle with nutmeg.

Sidecar

Cointreau is the best-known brand of the orange-flavored liqueur known generically as triple sec. It is drier and stronger than Curaçao and is always colorless.

4–6 cracked ice cubes
2 measures brandy
1 measure triple sec
1 measure lemon juice
orange peel twist,
to decorate

serves 1

❶ Put the ice into a cocktail shaker. Pour the brandy, triple sec, and lemon juice over the ice and shake vigorously until a frost forms.
❷ Strain into a chilled glass and decorate with the orange peel twist.

B and B

Although elaborate concoctions are great fun to mix—and drink—some of the best cocktails are the simplest. B and B—brandy and Bénédictine—couldn't be easier, but it has a superbly subtle flavor.

4–6 cracked ice cubes

1 measure brandy

1 measure Bénédictine

serves 1

❶ Put the ice cubes into a mixing glass. Pour the brandy and Bénédictine over the ice and stir to mix.

❷ Strain into a chilled cocktail glass.

Corpse Reviver

This cocktail is not designed to deal with a hangover the morning after, but it is a great pick-me-up after a busy day to get you in the mood to party. Note that it will not prevent your needing a different kind of corpse reviver the next day. This cocktail does not come with a medical guarantee.

4–6 cracked ice cubes
2 measures brandy
1 measure apple brandy
1 measure sweet vermouth

serves 1

❶ Put the cracked ice into a mixing glass. Pour the brandy, apple brandy, and vermouth over the ice. Stir gently to mix.
❷ Strain into a chilled cocktail glass.

Stinger

Aptly named, this is a refreshing, clean-tasting cocktail to tantalize the taste buds and make you sit up and take notice. However, bear in mind that it packs a punch and if you have too many, you are likely to keel over.

4–6 cracked ice cubes
2 measures brandy
1 measure white crème de menthe

serves 1

❶ Put the ice cubes into a cocktail shaker. Pour the brandy and crème de menthe over the ice. Shake vigorously until a frost forms.

❷ Strain into a small, chilled highball glass.

Between the Sheets

As the name of this cocktail always seems to imply romance and hints that the sheets in question are, at the very least, satin, make it for two people. Certainly, this delicious concoction is as smooth as silk.

8–10 cracked ice cubes

4 measures brandy

3 measures white rum

1 measure clear Curaçao

1 measure lemon juice

serves 2

❶ Put the cracked ice into a cocktail shaker. Pour the brandy, rum, Curaçao, and lemon juice over the ice. Shake vigorously until a frost forms.

❷ Strain into two chilled wine glasses or goblets.

American Rose

"A rose by any other name..."—this Oscar-winning cocktail has, rightly, inspired people around the world. It is truly a thing of beauty and a joy forever.

4-6 cracked ice cubes
1½ measures brandy
1 tsp grenadine
½ tsp Pernod
½ fresh peach, peeled and mashed
sparkling wine, to top off
fresh peach wedge, to decorate

serves 1

❶ Put the cracked ice in a cocktail shaker. Pour the brandy, grenadine, and Pernod over the ice and add the peach. Shake vigorously until a frost forms.

❷ Strain into a chilled wine goblet and top off with sparkling wine. Stir gently, then garnish with the peach wedge.

Mint Julep

A julep is simply a mixed drink sweetened with syrup—but the mere word conjures up images of ante-bellum cotton plantations and a long-gone, leisurely, and gracious way of life.

leaves of 1 fresh mint sprig
1 tbsp sugar syrup
(see page 11)
6–8 crushed ice cubes
3 measures bourbon whiskey
fresh mint sprig, to decorate

serves 1

❶ Put the mint leaves and sugar syrup into a small, chilled glass and mash with a teaspoon. Add crushed ice to fill the tumbler, then add the bourbon.

❷ Decorate with the mint sprig.

Whiskey Sour

Sours are short drinks, flavored with lemon or lime juice.
They can be made with almost any spirit, although
Whiskey Sour was the original and, for many, is still the
favorite version of this cocktail.

4–6 cracked ice cubes
2 measures American
blended whiskey
1 measure lemon juice
1 tsp sugar syrup
(see page 11)

To decorate
cocktail cherry
slice of orange

serves 1

❶ Put the cracked ice into
a cocktail shaker. Pour the
whiskey, lemon juice, and
sugar syrup over the ice.
Shake vigorously until a
frost forms.

❷ Strain into a chilled
cocktail glass and decorate
with the cocktail cherry and
orange slice.

Manhattan

Said to have been invented by Sir Winston Churchill's American mother, Jennie, the Manhattan is one of many cocktails named after places in New York City. The center of sophistication in the Jazz Age, the city is, once again, buzzing with cocktail bars for a new generation.

4–6 cracked ice cubes
dash of Angostura bitters
3 measures rye whiskey
1 measure sweet vermouth
cocktail cherry, to decorate

serves 1

❶ Put the cracked ice into a mixing glass. Dash the Angostura bitters over the ice and pour in the whiskey and vermouth. Stir well to mix.
❷ Strain into a chilled glass and decorate with the cherry.

Old Fashioned

So ubiquitous is this cocktail that a small, straight-sided tumbler is known as an old-fashioned glass. It is a perfect illustration of the saying, "Sometimes the old ones are the best."

sugar cube
dash of Angostura bitters
1 tsp water
2 measures bourbon
or rye whiskey
4–6 cracked ice cubes
lemon peel twist, to decorate

serves 1

❶ Place the sugar cube in a small, chilled Old Fashioned glass. Dash the bitters over the cube and add the water. Mash with a spoon until the sugar has dissolved.

❷ Pour the bourbon or rye whiskey into the glass and stir. Add the cracked ice cubes and then decorate with the lemon twist.

Boilermaker

Originally, boilermaker was slang for a shot of whiskey followed by a beer chaser. This version is marginally more sophisticated, but every bit as lethal.

1 cup English Pale Ale
1½ measures bourbon
or rye whiskey

serves 1

❶ Pour the beer into a chilled beer glass or tankard. Pour the bourbon or rye whiskey into a chilled shot glass.

❷ Gently submerge the shot glass in the beer.

Martini

For many, this is the ultimate cocktail. It is named after
its inventor, Martini de Anna de Toggia, and not the
famous brand of vermouth. The original version
comprised equal measures of gin and vermouth, now
known as a Fifty–Fifty, but the proportions vary, up to the
Ultra Dry Martini, when the glass is merely rinsed out
with vermouth before the gin is poured in.

4–6 cracked ice cubes
3 measures gin
1 tsp dry vermouth, or
to taste
cocktail olive, to decorate

serves 1

❶ Put the cracked ice cubes
into a mixing glass. Pour the
gin and vermouth over the ice
and stir well to mix.

❷ Strain into a chilled
cocktail glass and decorate
with a cocktail olive.

Bronx

Like Manhattan, the New York borough of the Bronx—and also the river of the same name—have been immortalized in cocktail bars throughout the world.

4–6 cracked ice cubes
2 measures gin
1 measure orange juice
½ measure dry vermouth
½ measure sweet vermouth

serves 1

❶ Put the cracked ice cubes into a mixing glass. Pour the gin, orange juice, and dry and sweet vermouth over the ice. Stir to mix.
❷ Strain into a chilled cocktail glass.

White Lady

Simple, elegant, subtle, and much more powerful than its appearance suggests, this is the perfect cocktail to serve before an *al fresco* summer dinner.

4–6 cracked ice cubes
2 measures gin
1 measure triple sec
1 measure lemon juice

serves 1

❶ Put the ice into a cocktail shaker. Pour the gin, triple sec, and lemon juice over the ice. Shake vigorously until a frost forms.

❷ Strain into a chilled cocktail glass.

Alexander

This creamy, chocolate-flavored, gin-based cocktail, decorated with grated nutmeg, is the head of quite an extended family of cocktails, which continues to grow.

4–6 cracked ice cubes
1 measure gin
1 measure crème de cacao
1 measure light cream
freshly grated nutmeg,
to decorate

serves 1

❶ Put the cracked ice cubes into a cocktail shaker. Pour the gin, crème de cacao, and light cream over the ice. Shake vigorously until a frost forms.

❷ Strain into a chilled cocktail glass and sprinkle with the nutmeg.

Tom Collins

This refreshing cocktail combines gin, lemon juice, and club soda to make a simple, cooling long drink. This is a venerable, classic cocktail, but the progenitor of several generations of the Collins family of drinks, scattered across the globe, was the popular John Collins cocktail.

5–6 cracked ice cubes
3 measures gin
2 measures lemon juice
½ measure sugar syrup
(see page 11)
club soda, to top off
slice of lemon, to decorate

serves 1

❶ Put the cracked ice into a cocktail shaker. Pour the gin, lemon juice, and sugar syrup over the ice. Shake vigorously until a frost forms.
❷ Strain into a tall, chilled tumbler and top off with club soda. Decorate with a slice of lemon.

Daisy

A Daisy is a long cocktail with a high proportion of alcohol and sweetened with fruit syrup. Perhaps it gets its name from the now old-fashioned slang when the word "daisy" referred to something exceptional and special.

4–6 cracked ice cubes
3 measures gin
1 measure lemon juice
1 tbsp grenadine
1 tsp sugar syrup
(see page 11)
club soda, to top off
slice of orange, to decorate

serves 1

❶ Put the cracked ice cubes into a cocktail shaker. Pour the gin, lemon juice, grenadine, and sugar syrup over the ice. Shake vigorously until a frost forms.

❷ Strain into a chilled highball glass and top off with club soda. Stir gently, then decorate with an orange slice.

Orange Blossom

It is disappointing to discover that the pretty name of this cocktail is derived from the practice of adding fresh orange juice to bathtub gin during the years of Prohibition in order to conceal its filthy flavor. Made with good-quality gin, which needs no such concealment, it is delightfully refreshing.

4–6 cracked ice cubes
2 measures gin
2 measures orange juice
slice of orange, to decorate

serves 1

❶ Put the cracked ice cubes into a cocktail shaker. Pour the gin and orange juice over the ice and shake vigorously until a frost forms.

❷ Strain into a chilled cocktail glass and decorate with the orange slice.

Club

Groucho Marx is well known for claiming that he wouldn't want to belong to any club that was prepared to accept him as a member. This Club and its many associates are unlikely ever to have any shortage of willing members.

4–6 cracked ice cubes
dash of yellow Chartreuse
2 measures gin
1 measure sweet vermouth

serves 1

❶ Put the cracked ice cubes into a mixing glass. Dash the Chartreuse over the ice and pour in the gin and vermouth. Stir well to mix.

❷ Strain into a chilled cocktail glass.

Rickey

The classic version of this cocktail is based on gin, but other spirits are also used, mixed with lime or lemon juice and club soda with no sweetening.

4–6 cracked ice cubes
2 measures gin
1 measure lime juice
club soda, to top off
slice of lemon, to decorate

serves 1

❶ Put the cracked ice cubes into a chilled highball glass or goblet. Pour the gin and lime juice over the ice. Top off with club soda.
❷ Stir gently to mix and decorate with the lemon slice.

Singapore Sling

In the days of the British Empire, the privileged would gather in the relative cool of the evening to refresh parched throats and gossip about the day's events at exclusive clubs. Those days are long gone, but a Singapore Sling is still the ideal thirst-quencher on hot summer evenings.

10–12 cracked ice cubes
2 measures gin
1 measure cherry brandy
1 measure lemon juice
1 tsp grenadine
club soda, to top off

To decorate
lime peel
cocktail cherries

serves 1

❶ Put 4–6 cracked ice cubes into a cocktail shaker. Pour the gin, cherry brandy, lemon juice, and grenadine over the ice. Shake vigorously until a frost forms.

❷ Half fill a chilled highball glass with cracked ice cubes and strain the cocktail over them. Top off with club soda and decorate with lime peel and cocktail cherries.

Long Island Iced Tea

Like many other classics, this cocktail dates from the days of Prohibition, when it was drunk from tea cups in an unconvincing attempt to fool the FBI that it was a harmless beverage.

10–12 cracked ice cubes
2 measures vodka
1 measure gin
1 measure white tequila
1 measure white rum
½ measure white crème de menthe
2 measures lemon juice
1 tsp sugar syrup (see page 11)
cola, to top off
wedge of lime or lemon, to decorate

❶ Put 4–6 cracked ice cubes into a cocktail shaker. Pour the vodka, gin, tequila, rum, crème de menthe, lemon juice, and sugar syrup over the ice. Shake vigorously until a frost forms.
❷ Half fill a tall, chilled Collins glass with cracked ice cubes and strain the cocktail over them. Top off with cola and decorate with the lime or lemon wedge.

serves 1

Dubarry

The Comtesse du Barry, the mistress of King Louis XV of France, was renowned for her extraordinary beauty. The guillotine brought an abrupt ending to her life—be careful not to lose your head over this delicious concoction.

4–6 cracked ice cubes
dash of Pernod
dash of Angostura bitters
2 measures gin
1 measure dry vermouth
lemon peel twist, to decorate

serves 1

❶ Put the ice cubes into a mixing glass and dash the Pernod and Angostura bitters over them. Pour in the gin and vermouth and stir well to mix.

❷ Strain into a chilled cocktail or wine glass and decorate with a twist of lemon.

Maiden's Blush

The name of this cocktail aptly describes its pretty color. Too many cocktails, however, and maidenly modesty may be abandoned and blushing could become compulsory.

4–6 cracked ice cubes

2 measures gin

½ tsp triple sec

½ tsp grenadine

½ tsp lemon juice

serves 1

❶ Put the cracked ice cubes into a cocktail shaker. Pour the gin, triple sec, grenadine, and lemon juice over the ice. Shake vigorously until a frost forms.

❷ Strain into a chilled cocktail glass or small highball glass.

Piña Colada

One of the younger generation of classics, this became
popular during the cocktail revival of the 1980s and has
remained so ever since.

4–6 crushed ice cubes

2 measures white rum

1 measure dark rum

3 measures pineapple juice

2 measures coconut cream

pineapple wedges, to decorate

serves 1

❶ Put the crushed ice into a
blender and add the white
rum, dark rum, pineapple
juice, and coconut cream.
Blend until smooth.

❷ Pour, without straining, into
a tall glass and decorate with
pineapple wedges speared on
a cocktail stick.

Acapulco

This is one of many cocktails that has changed from its original recipe over the years. To begin with, it was always rum-based and did not include any fruit juice. Nowadays, it is increasingly made with tequila, because this has become better known outside its native Mexico.

10–12 cracked ice cubes

2 measures white rum

½ measure triple sec

½ measure lime juice

1 tsp sugar syrup
(see page 11)

1 egg white

sprig of fresh mint,
to decorate

serves 1

❶ Put 4–6 cracked ice cubes into a cocktail shaker. Pour the rum, triple sec, lime juice, and sugar syrup over the ice and add the egg white. Shake vigorously until a frost forms.
❷ Half fill a chilled highball glass with cracked ice cubes and strain the cocktail over them. Decorate with the mint sprig.

Daiquiri

Daiquiri is a town in Cuba, where this drink was said to have been invented in the early part of the twentieth century. A businessman had run out of imported gin, so he had to make do with the local drink—rum—which, at that time, was of unreliable quality. To ensure that his guests would find it palatable he mixed it with other ingredients. This classic has since given rise to almost innumerable variations.

4–6 cracked ice cubes
2 measures white rum
¾ measure lime juice
½ tsp sugar syrup
(see page 11)

serves 1

❶ Put the cracked ice cubes into a cocktail shaker. Pour the rum, lime juice, and sugar syrup over the ice. Shake vigorously until a frost forms.
❷ Strain into a chilled cocktail glass.

Planter's Punch

**Derived from a Hindi word meaning five, punch is so
called because, traditionally, it contained five ingredients.**

10–12 cracked ice cubes

dash of grenadine

2 measures white rum

2 measures dark rum

1 measure lemon juice

1 measure lime juice

1 tsp sugar syrup (see page 11)

¼ tsp triple sec

sparkling mineral water

To decorate

slice of lemon

slice of lime

slice of pineapple

cocktail cherry

serves 1

❶ Put 4–6 cracked ice cubes
into a cocktail shaker. Dash
the grenadine over the ice
and pour in the white rum,
dark rum, lemon juice, lime
juice, sugar syrup, and triple
sec. Shake vigorously until a
frost forms.

❷ Half fill a tall, chilled
Collins glass with cracked ice
cubes and strain the cocktail
over them. Top off with
sparkling mineral water and
stir gently. Decorate with the
lemon, lime, and pineapple
slices and a cherry.

Cuba Libre

The 1960s and 1970s saw the meteoric rise in popularity of this simple, long drink, perhaps because of highly successful marketing by Bacardi brand rum, the original white Cuban rum (now produced in the Bahamas) and Coca-Cola, but more likely because rum and cola seem to be natural companions.

4–6 cracked ice cubes
2 measures white rum
cola, to top off
wedge of lime, to decorate

serves 1

❶ Half fill a highball glass with cracked ice cubes. Pour the rum over the ice and top off with cola.

❷ Stir gently to mix and decorate with a lime wedge.

Zombie

The individual ingredients of this cocktail, including liqueurs and fruit juices, can vary considerably.

4–6 crushed ice cubes

2 measures dark rum

2 measures white rum

1 measure golden rum

1 measure triple sec

1 measure lime juice

1 measure orange juice

1 measure pineapple juice

1 measure guava juice

1 tbsp grenadine

1 tbsp orgeat

1 tsp Pernod

fresh mint and pineapple, to decorate

serves 1

❶ Put the crushed ice cubes into a blender and add the three rums, triple sec, lime juice, orange juice, pineapple juice, guava juice, grenadine, orgeat, and Pernod. Blend until smooth.

❷ Pour, without straining, into a chilled Collins glass and decorate with the mint sprig and pineapple wedges.

Mai Tai

For some reason, this cocktail always inspires elaborate decoration with paper parasols, a selection of fruit, and spirals of citrus rind—sometimes you can be in danger of stabbing your nose on a cocktail stick.

4–6 cracked ice cubes
2 measures white rum
2 measures dark rum
1 measure clear Curaçao
1 measure lime juice
1 tbsp orgeat
1 tbsp grenadine

To decorate
paper parasol
slices of pineapple
cocktail cherries
orchid, optional

❶ Put the cracked ice cubes into a cocktail shaker. Pour the white and dark rums, Curaçao, lime juice, orgeat, and grenadine over the ice. Shake vigorously until a frost forms.

❷ Strain into a chilled Collins glass and decorate with the paper parasol, pineapple, and cherries, adding an orchid, if desired.

serves 1

Margarita

The traditional way to drink tequila is to shake a little salt on the back of your hand between the thumb and forefinger and, holding a wedge of lime or lemon, lick the salt, suck the fruit, and then down a shot of tequila in one. This cocktail, attributed to Francisco Morales and invented in 1942 in Mexico, is a more civilized version.

lime wedge
coarse salt
4–6 cracked ice cubes
3 measures white tequila
1 measure triple sec
2 measures lime juice
slice of lime, to decorate

serves 1

❶ Rub the rim of a chilled cocktail glass with the lime wedge and then dip in a saucer of coarse salt to frost.
❷ Put the cracked ice cubes into a cocktail shaker. Pour the tequila, triple sec, and lime juice over the ice. Shake vigorously until a frost forms.
❸ Strain into the prepared glass and decorate with the lime slice.

Tequila Sunrise

This is one cocktail you shouldn't rush when making, otherwise you will spoil the attractive sunrise effect as the grenadine slowly spreads through the orange juice.

4–6 cracked ice cubes
2 parts white tequila
orange juice, to top off
1 measure grenadine

serves 1

❶ Put the cracked ice cubes into a chilled highball glass. Pour the tequila over the ice and top off with the orange juice. Stir well to mix.
❷ Slowly pour in the grenadine and serve with a straw.

Brave Bull

Spain's historical associations with Mexico has left many legacies—not least a taste for bullfighting—although whether this cocktail is named in tribute to the animal or because it makes the drinker proverbially brave is anyone's guess.

4–6 cracked ice cubes
2 measures white tequila
1 measure Tia Maria
spiral of lemon peel,
to decorate

serves 1

❶ Put the cracked ice into a mixing glass. Pour the tequila and Tia Maria over the ice and stir well to mix.
❷ Strain into a chilled goblet and decorate with the spiral of lemon.

Bloody Mary

This classic cocktail was invented in 1921 at the legendary Harry's Bar in Paris. There are numerous versions—some much hotter and spicier than others.

4–6 cracked ice cubes
dash of Worcestershire sauce
dash of Tabasco sauce
2 measures vodka
6 measures tomato juice
juice of ½ lemon
pinch of celery salt
pinch of cayenne pepper

To decorate
celery stalk with leaves
slice of lemon

❶ Put the cracked ice into a cocktail shaker. Dash the Worcestershire sauce and Tabasco sauce over the ice and pour in the vodka, tomato juice, and lemon juice. Shake vigorously until a frost forms.
❷ Strain into a chilled rocks glass, add a pinch of celery salt and a pinch of cayenne, and decorate with a celery stalk and a slice of lemon.

serves 1

Black Russian

History records only White and Red Russians. The omission of the Black Russian is a sad oversight. For a coffee liqueur, you can use either Tia Maria or Kahlúa, depending on your personal taste—the latter is sweeter.

4–6 cracked ice cubes
2 measures vodka
1 measure coffee liqueur

serves 1

❶ Put the cracked ice cubes into a small, chilled highball glass. Pour the vodka and liqueur over the ice. Stir well to mix.

Moscow Mule

This cocktail came into existence through a happy coincidence during the 1930s. An American bar owner had overstocked with ginger beer, and a representative of a soda company invented the Moscow Mule to help him out of his difficulty.

10–12 cracked ice cubes
2 measures vodka
1 measure lime juice
ginger beer, to top off
slice of lime, to decorate

serves 1

❶ Put 4–6 cracked ice cubes into a cocktail shaker. Pour the vodka and lime juice over the ice. Shake vigorously until a frost forms.

❷ Half fill a chilled highball glass with cracked ice cubes and strain the cocktail over them. Top off with ginger beer. Decorate with a slice of lime.

Screwdriver

Always use freshly squeezed orange juice to make this refreshing cocktail—it is just not the same with bottled juice. This simple, classic cocktail has given rise to numerous and increasingly elaborate variations.

6–8 cracked ice cubes
2 measures vodka
orange juice, to top off
slice of orange, to decorate

serves 1

❶ Fill a chilled glass with cracked ice cubes. Pour the vodka over the ice and top off with orange juice.

❷ Stir well to mix and decorate with an orange slice.

Salty Dog

This is another cocktail that has changed since its invention. When it first appeared, gin-based cocktails were by far the most popular, but nowadays, a Salty Dog is more frequently made with vodka. You can use either spirit, but the cocktails will have different flavors.

1 tbsp granulated sugar

1 tbsp coarse salt

lime wedge

6–8 cracked ice cubes

2 measures vodka

grapefruit juice, to top off

serves 1

❶ Mix the sugar and salt in a saucer. Rub the rim of a chilled Collins glass with the lime wedge, then dip the tumbler in the sugar and salt mixture to frost.

❷ Fill the glass with cracked ice cubes and pour the vodka over them. Top off with grapefruit juice and stir to mix. Serve with a straw.

Grasshopper

This silky smooth, pale-green cocktail is enough to make anyone jump with delight. However, experts disagree on the original recipe and there seem to be at least three versions with the same name—as well as numerous variations. The recipe given here is also known as a Grasshopper Surprise.

4–6 cracked ice cubes

2 measures green crème de menthe

2 measures white crème de cacao

2 measures light cream

serves 1

❶ Put the cracked ice cubes into a cocktail shaker. Pour the crème de menthe, crème de cacao, and light cream over the ice. Shake vigorously until a frost forms.

❷ Strain into a chilled goblet.

Rhett Butler

When Margaret Mitchell wrote her long civil war story, *Gone With the Wind*, she created an enduring romantic hero in Rhett Butler. His debonair charm and devil-may-care lifestyle were brought alive by the heart-throb movie star Clark Gable.

4–6 cracked ice cubes
2 measures Southern Comfort
½ measure clear Curaçao
½ measure lime juice
1 tsp lemon juice
twist of lemon peel,
to decorate

serves 1

❶ Put the cracked ice cubes into a cocktail shaker. Pour the Southern Comfort, Curaçao, lime juice, and lemon juice over the ice. Shake vigorously until a frost forms.

❷ Strain into a chilled cocktail glass and decorate with the lemon twist.

Absinthe Friend

A popular cocktail ingredient, the *digestif* absinthe is no longer available. Flavored with wormwood, which it is said reacts with alcohol to cause brain damage, absinthe was banned by law in 1915. However, various pastis, including Pernod and Ricard, are still available and make good substitutes.

4–6 cracked ice cubes
dash of Angostura bitters
dash of sugar syrup
(see page 11)
1 measure Pernod
1 measure gin

serves 1

❶ Put the cracked ice cubes into a cocktail shaker. Dash the bitters and sugar syrup over the ice and pour in the Pernod and gin. Shake vigorously until a frost forms. ❷ Strain into a chilled glass.

Negroni

This aristocratic cocktail was created by Count Negroni at the Bar Giacosa in Florence, although since then, the proportions of gin to Campari have altered.

4–6 cracked ice cubes
1 measure Campari
1 measure gin
½ measure sweet vermouth
twist of orange peel,
to decorate

serves 1

❶ Put the cracked ice cubes into a mixing glass. Pour the Campari, gin, and vermouth over the ice. Stir well to mix.
❷ Strain into a chilled glass and decorate with the orange twist.

Rolls Royce

Hardly surprisingly, several classic cocktails have been named after this classic marque. This version was created by author H. E. Bates in his popular novel *The Darling Buds of May*.

4–6 cracked ice cubes
dash of orange bitters
2 measures dry vermouth
1 measure dry gin
1 measure Scotch whisky

serves 1

❶ Put the cracked ice cubes into a mixing glass. Dash the ice with the bitters.
❷ Pour the vermouth, gin, and whisky over the ice and stir to mix. Strain into a chilled cocktail glass.

Kir

As with the best mustard, crème de cassis production is centered on the French city of Dijon. This cocktail is named in commemoration of a partisan and mayor of the city, Félix Kir.

4–6 cracked ice cubes
2 measures crème de cassis
white wine, to top off
twist of lemon peel,
to decorate

serves 1

❶ Put the crushed ice cubes into a chilled wine glass. Pour the crème de cassis over the ice.
❷ Top off with chilled white wine and stir well. Decorate with the lemon twist.

Sherry Cobbler

A long drink made with syrup and fresh fruit
garnishes, Sherry Cobbler is the original, but there are
now numerous and often more potent variations.

6–8 cracked ice cubes
¼ tsp sugar syrup
(see page 11)
¼ tsp clear Curaçao
4 measures Amontillado
sherry

To decorate
pineapple wedges
twist of lemon peel

serves 1

❶ Fill a wine glass with
crushed ice. Add the sugar
syrup and Curaçao and stir
until a frost forms.
❷ Pour in the sherry and stir
well. Decorate with pineapple
wedges speared on a cocktail
stick and the lemon twist.

French 75

Although this cocktail was described in a cocktails book written in the early twentieth century as something that "definitely hits the spot," there seems to be some confusion about the actual ingredients. All recipes include champagne, but disagree about the spirits that should be included.

4–6 cracked ice cubes

2 measures brandy

1 measure lemon juice

1 tbsp sugar syrup

(see page 11)

chilled champagne, to top off

twist of lemon peel,

to decorate

serves 1

❶ Put the cracked ice cubes into a cocktail shaker. Pour the brandy, lemon juice, and sugar syrup over the ice and shake vigorously until a frost forms.

❷ Strain into a chilled highball glass and top off with champagne. Decorate with the lemon twist.

Buck's Fizz

Invented at Buck's Club in London, the original was invariably made with Bollinger champagne and it is true that the better the quality of the champagne, the better the flavor of the cocktail.

2 measures chilled
champagne
2 measures chilled
orange juice

serves 1

❶ Pour the champagne into a chilled champagne flute, then pour in the orange juice.

Contemporary Cocktails

Bosom Caresser

It would probably be unwise to investigate the provenance of this oddly named cocktail—perhaps it is so called because it creates a pleasantly warm glow in the cockles of the heart.

4–6 cracked ice cubes
dash of triple sec
1 measure brandy
1 measure Madeira

serves 1

❶ Put the cracked ice cubes into a mixing glass. Dash triple sec over the ice and pour in the brandy and Madeira.

❷ Stir well to mix, then strain into a chilled cocktail glass.

Adam's Apple

Applejack in the United States, Calvados in France, and apple brandy as a generic term—whatever you call it, its inclusion provides a delicious fruity flavor and a tempting aroma to this cocktail.

4-6 cracked ice cubes
dash of yellow Chartreuse
2 measures apple brandy
1 measure gin
1 measure dry vermouth

serves 1

❶ Put the cracked ice cubes into a mixing glass. Dash the Chartreuse over the ice and pour in the apple brandy, gin, and vermouth.

❷ Stir well to mix, then strain into a chilled glass.

Moonraker

A powerful mix, this cocktail is more likely to fire you into orbit than to reduce you to trying to rake the moon's reflection out of a pond.

4–6 cracked ice cubes
dash of Pernod
1 measure brandy
1 measure peach brandy
1 measure quinquina

serves 1

❶ Put the cracked ice cubes into a mixing glass. Dash Pernod over the ice and pour in the brandy, peach brandy, and quinquina.

❷ Stir well to mix, then strain into a chilled highball glass.

FBR

A number of cocktails are known simply by initials. In this case, FBR stands for Frozen Brandy and Rum. Others seem to be quite obscure and, in one or two instances, slightly naughty.

6–8 crushed ice cubes
2 measures brandy
1½ measures white rum
1 tbsp lemon juice
1 tsp sugar syrup
(see page 11)
1 egg white

❶ Put the crushed ice into a blender and add the brandy, rum, lemon juice, sugar syrup, and egg white. Blend until slushy.
❷ Pour the mixture into a chilled highball glass.

serves 1

Panda

Slivovitz is a colorless plum brandy, usually made from Mirabelle and Switzen plums. It is usually drunk straight, but can add a fruity note to cocktails. If it is not available, you could substitute apricot, peach, or cherry brandy—all fruits from the same family—but the cocktail will not look or taste quite the same.

4-6 cracked ice cubes
dash of sugar syrup
(see page 11)
1 measure slivovitz
1 measure apple brandy
1 measure gin
1 measure orange juice

serves 1

❶ Put the cracked ice cubes into a cocktail shaker. Dash the sugar syrup over the ice and pour in the slivovitz, apple brandy, gin, and orange juice. Shake vigorously until a frost forms.

❷ Strain into a chilled cocktail glass.

Honeymoon

The traditional nuptial journey is so called because the first month of marriage was thought to be sweet—and why not? If you are sick of the sight of champagne following the wedding, why not share this sweet concoction?

8–10 cracked ice cubes
4 measures apple brandy
2 measures Bénédictine
2 measures lemon juice
2 tsp triple sec

serves 2

❶ Put the cracked ice cubes into a cocktail shaker. Pour the brandy, Bénédictine, lemon juice, and triple sec over the ice. Shake vigorously until a frost forms.

❷ Strain into two chilled cocktail glasses.

Princess

No particular princess is specified, although a number of
other cocktails are named after queens and princes, as
well as princesses. Perhaps drinking this makes everyone
feel like royalty.

2 tsp chilled light cream

1 tsp superfine sugar

2 measures chilled
apricot brandy

serves 1

❶ Pour the cream into a small
bowl and stir in the sugar.
❷ Pour the apricot brandy
into a chilled liqueur glass
and float the sweetened
cream on top by pouring it
over the back of a teaspoon.

Highland Fling

Blended whisky is best suited to cocktails—single malts should always be drunk neat or simply with a little added mineral water. However, a throat-burning, harsh blend will make a mixture closer to rocket fuel than a cocktail and no amount of additional flavors will improve it.

4–6 cracked ice cubes
dash of Angostura bitters
2 measures Scotch whisky
1 measure sweet vermouth
cocktail olive, to decorate

serves 1

❶ Put the cracked ice into a mixing glass. Dash the ice with Angostura bitters. Pour the whisky and vermouth over the ice.

❷ Stir well to mix and strain into a chilled glass. Decorate with a cocktail olive.

Twin Peaks

Bourbon, named after a county in Kentucky, must be made from at least 51 percent corn mash and is America's most popular whiskey. It forms the basis of many more cocktails than its Scotch cousin.

4–6 cracked ice cubes
dash of triple sec
2 measures bourbon
1 measure Bénédictine
1 measure lime juice
slice of lime, to decorate

serves 1

❶ Put the cracked ice cubes into a cocktail shaker. Dash triple sec over the ice and pour in the bourbon, Bénédictine, and lime juice. Shake vigorously until a frost forms.

❷ Strain into a chilled highball glass and decorate with a slice of lime.

Irish Shillelagh

A shillelagh (pronounced *shee-lay-lee*) is a wooden cudgel, traditionally made from blackthorn. Undoubtedly, this is a cocktail that hits the spot.

4-6 crushed ice cubes

2 measures Irish whiskey

1 measure lemon juice

½ measure sloe gin

½ measure white rum

½ tsp sugar syrup
(see page 11)

½ peach, peeled, pitted, and
finely chopped

2 raspberries, to decorate

❶ Put the crushed ice cubes into a blender and add the whiskey, lemon juice, sloe gin, rum, sugar syrup, and chopped peach. Blend until smooth.

❷ Pour into a small, chilled highball glass and decorate with raspberries.

serves 1

Cowboy

In movies, cowboys drink their rye straight, often pulling the cork out of the bottle with their teeth, and it is certainly difficult to imagine John Wayne or Clint Eastwood sipping delicately from a chilled cocktail glass.

4–6 cracked ice cubes

3 measures rye whiskey

2 tbsp light cream

serves 1

❶ Put the cracked ice cubes into a cocktail shaker. Pour the whiskey and cream over the ice. Shake vigorously until a frost forms.

❷ Strain into a chilled highball glass.

Cat's Eye

A cat's eye is many things—besides what a cat sees with —including a semi-precious stone and a stripy marble. Now, it's a highly potent cocktail, as pretty as a gemstone and certainly more fun than playing marbles.

4–6 cracked ice cubes
2 measures gin
1½ measures dry vermouth
½ measure kirsch
½ measure triple sec
½ measure lemon juice
½ measure water

serves 1

❶ Put the cracked ice cubes into a cocktail shaker. Pour the gin, vermouth, kirsch, triple sec, lemon juice, and water over the ice.
❷ Shake vigorously until a frost forms. Strain into a chilled goblet.

Road Runner

Whether it is named after the real bird or after Bugs
Bunny's famous companion, this is a cocktail for slowing
down after a fast-moving day, not for speeding things up.

4–6 cracked ice cubes

2 measures gin

½ measure dry vermouth

½ measure Pernod

1 tsp grenadine

serves 1

❶ Put the cracked ice into a
cocktail shaker. Pour the gin,
vermouth, Pernod, and
grenadine over the ice. Shake
vigorously until a frost forms.
❷ Strain into a chilled
wine glass.

Breakfast

It is difficult to believe that anyone would actually have the stomach to cope with cocktails first thing in the morning—but then, for those who party all night and sleep all day, cocktail time coincides with breakfast.

4–6 cracked ice cubes
2 measures gin
1 measure grenadine
1 egg yolk

serves 1

❶ Put the cracked ice cubes into a cocktail shaker. Pour the gin and grenadine over the ice and add the egg yolk. Shake vigorously until a frost forms.

❷ Strain into a chilled highball glass.

Suffering Fool

You will have to make up your own mind whether this cocktail is a cure for someone already suffering or whether it is the cause of suffering still to come.

1 tbsp Angostura bitters
6–8 cracked ice cubes
2 measures gin
1½ measures brandy
½ measure lime juice
1 tsp sugar syrup
(see page 11)
ginger beer, to top off

To decorate
slice of cucumber
slice of lime
sprig of fresh mint

serves 1

❶ Pour the Angostura bitters into a chilled Collins glass and swirl around until the inside of the glass is coated. Pour out the excess and discard.

❷ Half fill the glass with cracked ice cubes. Pour the gin, brandy, lime juice, and sugar syrup over the ice. Stir well to mix.

❸ Top off with ginger beer and stir gently. Decorate with the cucumber and lime slices and a mint sprig.

What the Hell

Cheer yourself up when you are at a loose end, or when everything seems to have gone wrong, with this simple but delicious concoction.

4–6 cracked ice cubes
dash of lime juice
1 measure gin
1 measure apricot brandy
1 measure dry vermouth
twist of lemon peel,
to decorate

serves 1

❶ Put the cracked ice cubes into a mixing glass. Dash the lime juice over the ice and pour in the gin, apricot brandy, and vermouth. Stir well to mix.

❷ Strain into a chilled glass and decorate with a twist of lemon peel.

Nirvana

It may not be possible to obtain a perfect state of harmony and bliss through a cocktail, but this has to be the next best thing.

8–10 cracked ice cubes

2 measures dark rum

½ measure grenadine

½ measure tamarind syrup

1 tsp sugar syrup
(see page 11)

grapefruit juice, to top off

serves 1

❶ Put 4–6 cracked ice cubes into a cocktail shaker. Pour the rum, grenadine, tamarind syrup, and sugar syrup over the ice and shake vigorously until a frost forms.

❷ Half fill a chilled Collins glass with cracked ice cubes and then strain the cocktail over them. Top off with grapefruit juice.

Frozen Daiquiri

One of the great classic cocktails, the Daiquiri (see page 70) has moved on. It's not just mixed with fresh fruit or unusual ingredients, it's entered the twenty-first century with a whole new future, as slushes take on a leading role in fashionable cocktail bars.

6 crushed ice cubes
2 measures white rum
1 measure lime juice
1 tsp sugar syrup
(see page 11)
slice of lime, to decorate

serves 1

❶ Put the crushed ice into a blender and add the rum, lime juice, and sugar syrup. Blend until slushy.
❷ Pour into a chilled champagne flute and decorate with the lime slice.

Cinderella

If the fairy-story heroine had been knocking back cocktails until the clock struck midnight, it's hardly surprising that she forgot the time, mislaid her pumpkin, and lost her shoe on the way home.

4–6 cracked ice cubes
3 measures white rum
1 measure white port
1 measure lemon juice
1 tsp sugar syrup
(see page 11)
1 egg white

serves 1

❶ Put the cracked ice cubes into a cocktail shaker. Pour the rum, port, lemon juice, and sugar syrup over the ice and add the egg white.
❷ Shake vigorously until a frost forms and strain into a chilled glass.

Josiah's Bay Float

This is a wonderful cocktail for a special occasion in the summer. It's made for two to share, perhaps for an engagement party or a romantic *al fresco* dinner.

8–10 cracked ice cubes
2 measures golden rum
1 measure Galliano
2 measures pineapple juice
1 measure lime juice
4 tsp sugar syrup (see page 11)
champagne, to top off

To decorate
slices of lime
slices of lemon
cocktail cherries
To serve
scooped-out pineapple shell

1 Put the ice cubes into a cocktail shaker. Pour the rum, Galliano, pineapple juice, lime juice, and sugar syrup over the ice. Shake vigorously until a frost forms.

2 Strain into the pineapple shell, top off with champagne, and stir gently. Decorate with lime and lemon slices and cocktail cherries and serve with two straws.

serves 2

Palm Beach

If it's been a long time since your last vacation, conjure
up the blue skies of Florida and the rolling surf with this
bright and sunny cocktail.

4–6 cracked ice cubes

1 measure white rum

1 measure gin

1 measure pineapple juice

serves 1

❶ Put the cracked ice into a
cocktail shaker. Pour the rum,
gin, and pineapple juice over
the ice. Shake vigorously until
a frost forms.

❷ Strain into a chilled
highball glass.

Hayden's Milk Float

An irresistible melding of perfect partners—rum, cherry, chocolate, and cream—this rich cocktail tastes almost too good to be true.

4–6 cracked ice cubes
2 measures white rum
1 measure kirsch
1 measure white crème de cacao
1 measure light cream

To decorate
grated chocolate
cocktail cherry

serves 1

❶ Put the cracked ice cubes into a cocktail shaker. Pour the rum, kirsch, crème de cacao, and cream over the ice. Shake vigorously until a frost forms.

❷ Strain into a chilled highball glass. Sprinkle with grated chocolate and decorate with a cocktail cherry.

Bishop

It is strange how men of the cloth have gained a reputation for being enthusiastic about the good, material things in life. Even Rudyard Kipling wrote about smuggling "brandy for the parson." It goes to show that spirituality is no barrier to spirits.

4–6 cracked ice cubes
dash of lemon juice
1 measure white rum
1 tsp red wine
pinch of superfine sugar

serves 1

❶ Put the cracked ice cubes into a cocktail shaker. Dash the lemon juice over the ice, pour in the white rum and red wine, and add a pinch of sugar. Shake vigorously until a frost forms.

❷ Strain into a chilled wine glass.

El Diablo

One or two Diablos and you will certainly feel a bit of a devil, but one or two too many and you will end up feeling like the very devil.

6-8 cracked ice cubes
2-3 strips of lime peel
1 measure lime juice
3 measures white tequila
1 measure crème de cassis

serves 1

❶ Fill a small, chilled glass with cracked ice cubes and add the lime peel.
❷ Pour the lime juice over the ice and add the tequila and crème de cassis.

Huatusco Whammer

To be authentic, this cocktail should be topped off with Coca-Cola, but you can use other brands of cola if you prefer. Make sure that the cola is well chilled.

8–10 cracked ice cubes
1 measure white tequila
½ measure white rum
½ measure vodka
½ measure gin
½ measure triple sec
1 measure lemon juice
½ tsp sugar syrup
(see page 11)
cola, to top off

serves 1

❶ Put 4–6 cracked ice cubes into a cocktail shaker. Pour the tequila, rum, vodka, gin, triple sec, lemon juice, and sugar syrup over the ice. Shake vigorously until a frost forms.

❷ Fill a chilled Collins glass with cracked ice cubes and strain the cocktail over them. Top off with cola, stir gently, and serve with straws.

Coco Loco

This is a truly spectacular cocktail and can be great fun to decorate. Look out for swizzle sticks in the shape of palm trees or hula dancers and elaborately curly straws.

1 fresh coconut

8–10 crushed ice cubes

2 measures white tequila

1 measure gin

1 measure white rum

2 measures pineapple juice

1 tsp sugar syrup
(see page 11)

½ lime

serves 1

❶ Carefully saw the top off the coconut, reserving the liquid inside.

❷ Add the crushed ice, tequila, gin, rum, pineapple juice, and sugar syrup to the coconut, together with the reserved coconut liquid.

❸ Squeeze the lime over the cocktail and drop it in. Stir well and serve with a straw.

Tequila Mockingbird

In spite of the horrible literary pun in the name, this popular cocktail is fast becoming a modern classic.

4–6 cracked ice cubes
2 measures white tequila
1 measure white crème de menthe
1 measure fresh lime juice

serves 1

❶ Put the cracked ice cubes into a cocktail shaker. Add the tequila, crème de menthe, and lime juice. Shake vigorously until a frost forms.
❷ Strain into a chilled highball glass.

Tequila Slammer

Slammers, also known as shooters, are currently very fashionable. The idea is that you pour the different ingredients directly into the glass, without stirring (some slammers form colorful layers). Cover the top of the glass with one hand to prevent spillage, then slam the glass on the bar or a table to mix, and drink the cocktail down in one. It is essential to use a strong glass that is unlikely to break under such treatment.

1 measure white tequila
1 measure lemon juice
chilled sparkling wine, to
top off

serves 1

❶ Put the tequila and lemon juice into a chilled glass and stir to mix. Top off with sparkling wine.

❷ Cover the glass with your hand and slam.

Wild Night Out

Tequila has a reputation for being an extraordinarily potent spirit, but most commercially exported brands are the same standard strength as other spirits, such as gin or whiskey. "Home-grown" tequila or its close relative, mescal, may be another matter.

4–6 cracked ice cubes
3 measures white tequila
2 measures cranberry juice
1 measure lime juice
club soda, to top off

serves 1

❶ Put the cracked ice cubes into a cocktail shaker. Pour the tequila, cranberry juice, and lime juice over the ice. Shake vigorously until a frost forms.

❷ Half fill a chilled highball glass with cracked ice cubes and strain the cocktail over them. Add club soda to taste.

Carolina

White tequila is most commonly used for mixing cocktails, but some require the mellower flavor of the amber-colored, aged tequilas, which are known as golden tequila or *añejo*.

4–6 cracked ice cubes
3 measures golden tequila
1 tsp grenadine
1 tsp vanilla extract
1 measure light cream
1 egg white

To decorate
ground cinnamon
cocktail cherry

serves 1

❶ Put the cracked ice cubes into a cocktail shaker. Pour the tequila, grenadine, vanilla, and cream over the ice and add the egg white. Shake vigorously until a frost forms.
❷ Strain into a chilled cocktail glass. Sprinkle with cinnamon and decorate with a cocktail cherry.

Chili Willy

Truly a cocktail for the brave-hearted—the heat depends on the amount of chile included and whether it is deseeded first. It's a popular misconception that the heat of a chile is mainly in the seeds. In fact, the seeds contain no capsaicin—the heat factor—at all, but it is mostly concentrated in the flesh surrounding them. Deseeding the chiles removes most of this intensely hot flesh.

4–6 cracked ice cubes
2 measures vodka
1 tsp chopped fresh chile

serves 1

❶ Put the ice into a cocktail shaker. Pour the vodka over the ice and add the chile.
❷ Shake until a frost forms and strain into a chilled glass.

Crocodile

This is certainly a snappy cocktail with a bit of bite. However, it probably gets its name from its spectacular color—Midori, a Japanese melon-flavored liqueur, is a startling shade of green.

4–6 cracked ice cubes
2 measures vodka
1 measure triple sec
1 measure Midori
2 measures lemon juice

serves 1

❶ Put the cracked ice cubes into a cocktail shaker. Pour the vodka, triple sec, Midori, and lemon juice over the ice. Shake vigorously until a frost forms.

❷ Strain into a chilled cocktail glass.

Grimace and Grin

Cocktails flavored with candies are very fashionable, which is probably a good indication of how enthusiastically a new, young generation is rediscovering the joys of mixed drinks.

¾ cup sharp-flavored jellybeans, such as sour cherry, lemon, and apple

¾ bottle vodka, about 2¼ cups

serves 15–20

❶ Reserve ¼ cup of the jellybeans and place the remainder in a microwave-proof or heatproof bowl. Add about 4 tablespoons of the vodka. Either microwave until the jellybeans have melted or set the bowl over a pan of barely simmering water and heat until the beans have melted.

❷ Pour the mixture through a funnel into the vodka remaining in the bottle and add the reserved jellybeans. Replace the cap and chill in the refrigerator for at least 2 hours.

❸ To serve, shake the bottle vigorously, then pour into chilled cocktail glasses.

Polynesian Pepper Pot

It may seem strange to make a sweet drink and then season it with pepper and spices, but there is a long and honorable culinary tradition of making the most of the slightly acerbic flavor of pineapple in this kind of way.

4–6 cracked ice cubes

dash of Tabasco sauce

2 measures vodka

1 measure golden rum

4 measures pineapple juice

½ measure orgeat

1 tsp lemon juice

¼ tsp cayenne pepper

pinch of curry powder,
to decorate

❶ Put the cracked ice into a cocktail shaker. Dash Tabasco sauce over the ice, pour in the vodka, rum, pineapple juice, orgeat, and lemon juice and add the cayenne. Shake vigorously until a frost forms. ❷ Strain into a chilled glass and sprinkle curry powder on top.

serves 1

Fuzzy Navel

This is another one of those cocktails with a name that plays on the ingredients—fuzzy to remind you that it contains peach schnapps and navel because it is mixed with orange juice. It is not intended as a reflection on anyone's personal hygiene.

4–6 cracked ice cubes
2 measures vodka
1 measure peach schnapps
1 cup orange juice
slice of orange, to decorate

serves 1

❶ Put the cracked ice cubes into a cocktail shaker. Pour the vodka, peach schnapps, and orange juice over the ice. Shake vigorously until a frost forms.

❷ Strain into a chilled glass and then decorate with a slice of orange.

Vodga

As a rule, classic cocktails based on vodka were intended
to provide the kick of an alcoholic drink with no tell-tale
signs on the breath and they were usually fairly simple
mixes of fruit juice, sodas, and other nonalcoholic
flavorings. By contrast, contemporary cocktails based on
vodka often include other aromatic and flavorsome spirits
and liqueurs, with vodka adding extra strength.

4–6 cracked ice cubes
2 measures vodka
1 measure Strega
½ measure orange juice

serves 1

❶ Put the cracked ice cubes
into a cocktail shaker. Pour
the vodka, Strega, and orange
juice over the ice. Shake
vigorously until a frost forms.
❷ Strain into a chilled
cocktail glass.

Mudslide

This ominous-sounding cocktail is actually a gorgeously creamy and richly-flavored concoction that is delicious whatever the weather conditions.

4–6 cracked ice cubes
1½ measures Kahlúa
1½ measures Bailey's Irish Cream
1½ measures vodka

serves 1

❶ Put the cracked ice cubes into a cocktail shaker. Pour the Kahlúa, Bailey's Irish Cream, and vodka over the ice. Shake vigorously until a frost forms.
❷ Strain into a chilled goblet.

Godfather

Amaretto is an Italian liqueur, so perhaps the inspiration for this cocktail comes from Don Corleone, the eponymous character in Mario Puzo's best-selling novel, unforgettably portrayed in the movie by Marlon Brando.

4–6 cracked ice cubes
2 measures Scotch whisky
1 measure amaretto

serves 1

❶ Fill a chilled highball glass with cracked ice cubes. Pour in the whisky and amaretto and stir to mix.

Freedom Fighter

Crème Yvette is an American liqueur flavored with Parma violets. Because it has such a distinctive taste, you either love it or hate it—but it certainly makes pretty cocktails because it is such a lovely color. You could also use crème de violette instead of Crème Yvette, which has a similar although not identical appearance.

4–6 cracked ice cubes
3 measures sloe gin
1 measure Crème Yvette
1 measure lemon juice
1 egg white

serves 1

❶ Put the cracked ice cubes into a cocktail shaker. Pour the gin, Crème Yvette, and lemon juice over the ice and add the egg white. Shake vigorously until a frost forms.

❷ Strain the mixture into a chilled wine glass.

Banshee

A surprising number of cocktails are named after ghouls, ghosts, and things that go bump in the night. It seems unlikely that this one will get you wailing (except with delight), but it might make your hair stand on end.

4–6 cracked ice cubes
2 measures crème de banane
1 measure crème de cacao
1 measure light cream

serves 1

❶ Put the cracked ice cubes into a cocktail shaker. Pour the crème de banane, crème de cacao, and light cream over the ice. Shake vigorously until a frost forms.
❷ Strain into a chilled wine glass.

Angel's Delight

This is a modern version of the classic pousse café, an unmixed, mixed drink, in that the ingredients form separate layers in the glass—provided you have a steady hand—to create a rainbow effect. You can drink this cocktail as a slammer (see page 170) or sip it in a more genteel manner.

½ measure chilled grenadine
½ measure chilled triple sec
½ measure chilled sloe gin
½ measure chilled
light cream

serves 1

❶ Pour the grenadine into a chilled shot glass, pousse café glass, or champagne flute, then, with a steady hand, pour in the triple sec to make a second layer.

❷ Add the sloe gin to make a third layer and, finally, add the cream to float on top.

Pink Squirrel

Crème de noyaux has a wonderful, slightly bitter, nutty flavor, but is, in fact, made from peach and apricot kernels. It is usually served as a liqueur, but does combine well with some other ingredients in cocktails.

4–6 cracked ice cubes
2 measures dark crème de cacao
1 measure crème de noyaux
1 measure light cream

serves 1

❶ Put the cracked ice cubes into a cocktail shaker. Pour the crème de cacao, crème de noyaux, and light cream over the ice. Shake vigorously until a frost forms.

❷ Strain into a chilled cocktail glass.

Full Monty

The expression "full monty," meaning not holding anything back, has been around for a long time, but was given a new lease of life by the highly successful British movie of the same title. However, you can keep your clothes on when mixing and drinking this cocktail.

4–6 cracked ice cubes
1 measure vodka
1 measure Galliano
grated ginseng root,
to decorate

serves 1

❶ Put the cracked ice cubes into a cocktail shaker. Pour the vodka and Galliano over the ice. Shake vigorously until a frost forms.
❷ Strain into a chilled cocktail glass and sprinkle with grated ginseng root.

Star Bangled Spanner

Although only half measures of each spirit are used, there are seven layers of them, so this is quite a potent cocktail. It is probably fortunate that after getting your tongue around a couple, your hand will become too unsteady to pour more.

½ measure chilled
green Chartreuse
½ measure chilled triple sec
½ measure chilled
cherry brandy
½ measure chilled
crème violette
½ measure chilled
yellow Chartreuse
½ measure chilled
blue Curaçao
½ measure chilled brandy

❶ Pour the green Chartreuse into a chilled champagne flute, then, with a steady hand, gently pour in the triple sec to make a second layer. ❷ Gently add the cherry brandy to make a third layer, the crème violette to make a fourth, the yellow Chartreuse to make a fifth, and the Curaçao to make a sixth. ❸ Finally, float the brandy on top.

serves 1

Mad Dog

This cocktail is named in honor of Maximum Dog, who is himself a cocktail of breeds and who has been described as a cross between a goat and a monkey. However, he is not allowed to drink it.

4–6 cracked ice cubes
1 measure white tequila
1 measure crème de banane
1 measure white crème
de cacao
½ measure lime juice

To decorate
slice of lime
slice of banana
cocktail cherry

❶ Put the cracked ice cubes into a cocktail shaker. Pour the tequila, crème de banane, crème de cacao, and lime juice over the ice. Shake vigorously until a frost forms.
❷ Strain into a chilled cocktail glass and decorate with a lime slice, banana slice, and cocktail cherry.

serves 1

John Wood

Vermouth is an immensely useful flavoring for cocktails, because it contains more than fifty herbs and spices, ranging from cloves to rose petals, and combines well with many spirits, most notably gin. However, it has fallen in popularity as a base for cocktails over the last decade, but is now enjoying a revival of interest.

4–6 cracked ice cubes
dash of Angostura bitters
2 measures sweet vermouth
½ measure kümmel
½ measure Irish whiskey
1 measure lemon juice

serves 1

❶ Put the cracked ice cubes into a cocktail shaker. Dash Angostura bitters over the ice and pour in the vermouth, kümmel, whiskey, and lemon juice. Shake vigorously until a frost forms.

❷ Strain into a chilled wine glass.

Which Way

Anise-flavored pastis, such as Pernod, are firm favorites in today's cocktail bars and often form the basis of almost lethally strong drinks.

4–6 cracked ice cubes
1 measure Pernod
1 measure Anisette
1 measure brandy

serves 1

❶ Put the cracked ice cubes into a cocktail shaker. Pour the Pernod, Anisette, and brandy over the ice. Shake vigorously until a frost forms.
❷ Strain into a chilled wine glass.

Jade

You can tell good jade because it always feel cold to the touch—and that should apply to cocktails, too. No cocktail bar—whether in a hotel, pub, or at home—can ever have too much ice. Don't forget to chill the champagne for at least 2 hours before mixing.

4–6 cracked ice cubes
dash of Angostura bitters
¼ measure Midori
¼ measure blue Curaçao
¼ measure lime juice
chilled champagne, to top off
slice of lime, to decorate

serves 1

❶ Put the cracked ice cubes into a cocktail shaker. Dash Angostura bitters over the ice and pour in the Midori, Curaçao, and lime juice. Shake vigorously until a frost forms.
❷ Strain into a chilled champagne flute, top off with chilled champagne and decorate with a slice of lime.

Caribbean Champagne

Both rum and bananas are naturally associated with the tropics, but wine does not spring so readily to mind when the Caribbean is mentioned. However, remember that France and many Caribbean islands, such as Martinique and Guadeloupe, share a long history.

½ measure white rum
½ measure crème de banane
chilled champagne, to top off
slices of banana, to decorate

serves 1

❶ Pour the rum and crème de banane into a chilled champagne flute. Top off with champagne.

❷ Stir gently to mix and decorate with banana slices.

Millennium Cocktail

A good way to start the twenty-first century—and an even better way to carry on—is to drink this sparkling cocktail at regular intervals.

4–6 cracked ice cubes
1 measure raspberry vodka
1 measure fresh
raspberry juice
1 measure orange juice
chilled champagne, to top off
raspberries, to decorate

serves 1

❶ Put the cracked ice cubes into a cocktail shaker. Pour the vodka, raspberry juice, and orange juice over the ice. Shake vigorously until a frost forms.

❷ Strain into a chilled champagne flute and top off with chilled champagne. Stir gently to mix and decorate with raspberries.

Nonalcoholic Cocktails

Lip Smacker

So many delicious ingredients are available today, that nonalcoholic cocktails really have come into their own. This one has all the kick of an alcoholic cocktail.

4–6 crushed ice cubes
1 small tomato, peeled, deseeded, and chopped
1 measure orange juice
2 tsp lime juice
1 scallion, chopped
1 small fresh red chile, deseeded and chopped
pinch of superfine sugar
pinch of salt
dash of Tabasco sauce
slice of lime and a chile rosette, to decorate

❶ Put the crushed ice, tomato, orange juice, lime juice, scallion, and chile in a blender and process until smooth.

❷ Pour into a chilled glass, season to taste with sugar, salt, and Tabasco sauce and stir to mix. Decorate with a slice of lime and a chile rosette.

serves 1

Bloody January

Generally, the best nonalcoholic cocktails are originals rather than pale and often insipid copies of their traditional, alcoholic cousins. This nonalcoholic version of the Bloody Mary is one of the exceptions and has some of the kick of the classic cocktail.

4–6 crushed ice cubes
1 medium red bell pepper, deseeded
and coarsely chopped
2 large tomatoes, peeled, deseeded, and
coarsely chopped
1 fresh green chile, deseeded
juice of 1 lime
salt and freshly ground black pepper
celery stalk, to decorate

❶ Put the crushed ice cubes into a blender and add the red bell pepper, tomatoes, chile, and lime juice. Blend until smooth.
❷ Pour into a chilled highball glass and season to taste with salt and pepper. Decorate with a celery stalk.

serves 1

Carrot Cream

Although they are vegetables, carrots have a strong hint of sweetness that makes them or their juice an excellent and delicious basis for mixed drinks. Since raw carrots are packed with vitamins and minerals, this is a healthy and nutritious option, too.

4-6 cracked ice cubes
2 measures carrot juice
2½ measures light cream
1 measure orange juice
1 egg yolk
slice of orange, to decorate

serves 1

❶ Put the cracked ice cubes into a cocktail shaker. Pour the carrot juice, cream, and orange juice over the ice and add the egg yolk. Shake vigorously until a frost forms.
❷ Strain into a chilled glass and decorate with the orange slice.

Clam Digger

This is another good cocktail for a Sunday brunch, when alcoholic drinks can be too soporific and you end up wasting the rest of the day, but you still want something to wake up the tastebuds and set them tingling.

10–12 cracked ice cubes
Tabasco sauce
Worcestershire sauce
4 measures tomato juice
4 measures clam juice
¼ tsp horseradish sauce
celery salt and freshly ground black pepper

To decorate
celery stalk
wedge of lime

serves 1

❶ Put 4–6 cracked ice cubes into a cocktail shaker. Dash the Tabasco sauce and Worcestershire sauce over the ice, pour in the tomato juice and clam juice, and add the horseradish sauce. Shake vigorously until a frost forms.

❷ Fill a chilled Collins glass with cracked ice cubes and strain the cocktail over them. Season to taste with celery salt and pepper and decorate with a celery stalk and lime wedge.

Faux Kir

A nonalcoholic version of a classic wine cocktail, this drink is just as colorful and tasty. French and Italian fruit syrups are often the best quality and have the most intense flavor.

1 measure chilled
raspberry syrup
chilled white grape juice,
to top off
twist of lemon peel,
to decorate

serves 1

❶ Pour the raspberry syrup into a chilled wine glass. Top off with the grape juice.
❷ Stir well to mix and then decorate with the lemon twist.

Eye of the Hurricane

In recent years, a vast range of fruit juices and syrups has become widely available. These can extend the range of the cocktail bar and are particularly useful for nonalcoholic mixed drinks, which were once heavily dependent on the somewhat tired old favorites of orange, lemon, and lime juices.

4–6 cracked ice cubes
2 measures passion fruit syrup
1 measure lime juice
bitter lemon, to top off
slice of lemon, to decorate

serves 1

❶ Put the cracked ice cubes into a mixing glass. Pour the syrup and lime juice over the ice and stir well to mix.

❷ Strain into a chilled highball glass and top off with bitter lemon. Stir gently and decorate with the lemon slice.

Juicy Julep

Taken from the Arabic word, meaning a rose syrup, it seems likely that this was always intended to be a nonalcoholic drink and that it was bourbon-drinkers who hijacked the term, not the other way around. (For an alcoholic variation, see Mint Julep, page 30.)

4–6 cracked ice cubes
1 measure orange juice
1 measure pineapple juice
1 measure lime juice
½ measure raspberry syrup
4 crushed fresh mint leaves
ginger ale, to top off
sprig of fresh mint,
to decorate

serves 1

❶ Put the cracked ice cubes into a cocktail shaker. Pour the orange juice, pineapple juice, lime juice, and raspberry syrup over the ice and add the mint leaves. Shake vigorously until a frost forms.

❷ Strain into a chilled Collins glass, top off with ginger ale, and stir gently. Decorate with a fresh mint sprig.

Island Cooler

Nothing could be more refreshing on a hot summer's day
than this colorful combination of tropical fruit juices.
To get into a party mood, go to town with the decoration
with a cocktail parasol, swizzle stick, and straws, as well
as fresh fruit, if you like.

8–10 cracked ice cubes
2 measures orange juice
1 measure lemon juice
1 measure pineapple juice
1 measure papaya juice
½ tsp grenadine
sparkling mineral water,
to top off

To decorate
pineapple wedges
cocktail cherries

serves 1

❶ Put 4–6 cracked ice cubes
into a cocktail shaker. Pour
the fruit juices and the
grenadine over the ice. Shake
vigorously until a frost forms.
❷ Half fill a chilled Collins
glass with cracked ice cubes
and pour the cocktail over
them. Top off with sparkling
mineral water and stir gently.
Decorate with pineapple
wedges and cocktail cherries
speared on a cocktail stick.

Little Prince

Sparkling apple juice is a particularly useful ingredient in nonalcoholic cocktails because it adds flavor and color, as well as fizz. Try using it as a substitute for champagne in nonalcoholic versions of such cocktails as Buck's Fizz (see page 112).

4–6 cracked ice cubes

1 measure apricot juice

1 measure lemon juice

2 measures sparkling
apple juice

twist of lemon peel,
to decorate

serves 1

❶ Put the cracked ice cubes into a mixing glass. Pour the apricot juice, lemon juice and apple juice over the ice and stir well.

❷ Strain into a chilled highball glass and decorate with the lemon twist.

Sparkling Peach Melba

Peach Melba was a dessert invented by Escoffier, chef at the Savoy Hotel, in honor of the Australian opera singer Dame Nellie Melba. This simple, but perfect partnership of peaches and raspberries has become a classic combination, now transformed into a wonderfully refreshing cocktail.

¼ cup frozen raspberries
4 measures peach juice
sparkling mineral water,
to top off

serves 1

❶ Rub the raspberries through a wire strainer with the back of a wooden spoon. Transfer the purée to a cocktail shaker.

❷ Pour the peach juice into the cocktail shaker and shake vigorously until a frost forms.

❸ Strain into a tall, chilled tumbler and top off with sparkling mineral water. Stir gently.

California Smoothie

Smoothies of all sorts—alcoholic and nonalcoholic—have become immensely popular in the last two or three years. The secret of success is to blend them on medium speed until just smooth.

1 banana, peeled and
thinly sliced
½ cup strawberries
½ cup pitted dates
4½ tsp honey
1 cup orange juice
4–6 crushed ice cubes

serves 1

❶ Put the banana, strawberries, dates, and honey into a blender and blend until smooth.
❷ Add the orange juice and crushed ice cubes and blend again until smooth. Pour into a chilled Collins glass.

Italian Soda

Available from Italian delicatessens and some supermarkets, Italian syrup comes in a wide variety of flavors, including a range of fruit and nuts. French syrups are similar and also include many different flavors. You can substitute your favorite for the hazelnut used here and vary the quantity depending on how sweet you like your drinks.

6–8 cracked ice cubes
1–1½ measures hazelnut syrup
sparkling mineral water, to top off
slice of lime, to decorate

❶ Fill a chilled Collins glass with cracked ice cubes. Pour the hazelnut syrup over the ice and top off with sparkling mineral water.

❷ Stir gently and decorate with the lime slice.

serves 1

Grapefruit Cooler

This is a wonderfully refreshing drink that is ideal for serving at a family barbecue. Start making this at least two hours before you want to serve it to allow plenty of time for the mint to steep in the syrup.

2 oz/60 g fresh mint
2 measures sugar syrup
(see page 11)
2 cups grapefruit juice
4 measures lemon juice
about 30 cracked ice cubes
sparkling mineral water,
to top off
sprigs of fresh mint,
to decorate

serves 6

❶ Crush the mint leaves. Put in a small bowl with the sugar syrup and stir well. Set aside for 2 hours. Mash with a spoon from time to time.

❷ Strain into a pitcher. Add the grapefruit juice and lemon juice. Cover with plastic wrap and chill for 2 hours.

❸ To serve, fill six chilled Collins glasses with cracked ice. Divide the cocktail among the glasses and top off with sparkling mineral water. Decorate with mint sprigs.

Cranberry Punch

A sophisticated punch, this drink is delicious served hot for a winter party. It is particularly good for celebrating the New Year, especially if you have to drive home.

2½ cups cranberry juice
2½ cups orange juice
⅔ water
½ tsp ground ginger
¼ tsp ground cinnamon
¼ tsp freshly grated nutmeg
slices of lemon and orange, to decorate

serves 10

❶ Put the cranberry juice, orange juice, water, ginger, cinnamon, and nutmeg in a pan and bring to a boil. Lower the heat and simmer for 5 minutes.

❷ Remove the pan from the heat. Ladle into warmed individual punch glasses or pour into a warmed punch bowl. Decorate with slices of lemon and orange.

Mocha Slush

Definitely for people with a sweet tooth, this is a
chocoholic's dream and is popular with adults, as well
as children.

4–6 crushed ice cubes

2 measures coffee syrup

1 measure chocolate syrup

4 measures milk

grated chocolate, to decorate

serves 1

❶ Put the crushed ice cubes
into a blender and add the
coffee syrup, chocolate syrup,
and milk. Blend until slushy.

❷ Pour into a chilled
goblet and sprinkle with
grated chocolate.

Shirley Temple

This is one of the most famous of classic nonalcoholic cocktails. Shirley Temple Black became a respected diplomat, but this cocktail dates from the days when she was an immensely popular child movie star in the 1930s.

8–10 cracked ice cubes
2 measures lemon juice
½ measure grenadine
½ measure sugar syrup
(see page 11)
ginger ale, to top off

To decorate
slice of orange
cocktail cherry

serves 1

❶ Put 4–6 cracked ice cubes into a cocktail shaker. Pour the lemon juice, grenadine, and sugar syrup over the ice and shake vigorously.

❷ Half fill a small, chilled glass with cracked ice cubes and strain the cocktail over them. Top off with ginger ale. Decorate with an orange slice and a cocktail cherry.

Soft Sangria

This is a version of the well-known Spanish wine cup that has caught out many an unwary tourist with its potency. A Soft Sangria poses no such danger.

6 cups red grape juice

1¼ cups orange juice

3 measures cranberry juice

2 measures lemon juice

2 measures lime juice

4 measures sugar syrup (see page 11)

block of ice

To decorate

slices of lemon

slices of orange

slices of lime

serves 20

❶ Put the grape juice, orange juice, cranberry juice, lemon juice, lime juice, and sugar syrup into a chilled punch bowl and stir well.

❷ Add the ice and decorate with the slices of lemon, orange, and lime.

Melon Medley

Choose a very ripe, sweet-fleshed melon, such as a cantaloupe, for this lovely, fresh-tasting cocktail. This melon drink is perfect for sipping on a hot summer's evening.

4–6 crushed ice cubes
½ cup melon flesh
4 measures orange juice
½ measure lemon juice

serves 1

❶ Put the crushed ice cubes into a blender and add the diced melon. Pour in the orange juice and lemon juice. Blend until slushy.

❷ Pour the mixture into a chilled Collins glass.

Glossary

Amaretto: almond-flavored liqueur

Amer Picon: French apéritif bitters, flavored with orange and gentian

Angostura bitters: rum-based bitters from Trinidad

Anisette: French liqueur, flavored with anise, and other herbs

Applejack: North American name for apple brandy

Aquavit: Scandinavian grain spirit, usually flavored with caraway

Armagnac: French brandy rarely used for cocktails

Bailey's Irish Cream: Irish, whiskey-based liqueur

Bénédictine: French, monastic liqueur flavored with herbs, spices, and honey

Bitters: a flavor-enhancer made from berries, roots, and herbs

Bourbon: American whiskey made from a mash that must contain at least 51 percent corn

Calvados: French apple brandy from Normandy

Chartreuse: French monastic liqueur flavored with herbs—green Chartreuse is stronger than yellow

Cobbler: a long, mixed drink once based on sherry but now made from other ingredients

Crème de banane: banana-flavored liqueur

Crème de cacao: French, chocolate-flavored liqueur

Crème de cassis: blackcurrant-flavored liqueur

Crème de framboise: raspberry-flavored liqueur

Crème de menthe: mint-flavored liqueur—may be white or green

Crème de noyaux: liqueur made from apricot and peach kernels

Crème violette: violet-flavored liqueur

Crème Yvette: American Parma violet-flavored liqueur

Curaçao: clear orange-flavored liqueur, also available in orange and blue

Drambuie: Scotch whisky-based liqueur, flavored with honey and heather

Eau-de-vie: spirit distilled from fruit

Falernum: Caribbean syrup flavored with fruit and spices

Fernet Branca: Italian bitter liqueur

Flip: spirit based, creamy drink with egg

Fruit Brandy: strictly speaking, brandy is distilled from fermented grapes, but many fruit brandies are distilled from whatever the fruit type is, such as apple and apricot. Plum brandy, also known as slivovitz, is usually made from Mirabelle and Switzen plums

Galliano: Italian liqueur, flavored with honey and vanilla

Genever: also known as Hollands and Dutch gin, the original gin, which is sweeter and fuller-flavored than London, Plymouth, or dry gin—is rarely used in cocktails

Gomme Syrup: sweet syrup from France

Grand Marnier: French, orange flavored, Cognac-based liqueur

Grappa: fiery, Italian spirit distilled from wine must

Grenadine: nonalcoholic pomegranate-flavored syrup—used to sweeten and color cocktails

Julep: originally a sweet

syrup, now a family of spirit-based cocktails, flavored and decorated with fresh mint

Kahlúa: Mexican brand of coffee liqueur

Kirsch: colorless cherry-flavored eau-de-vie

Kümmel: colorless Dutch liqueur, flavored with caraway

Lillet: French herb-flavored liqueur, based on wine and Armagnac

Madeira: fortified wine from Madeira

Malibu: coconut liqueur based on rum

Mandarine Napoléon: Belgian, brandy-based liqueur flavored with tangerines

Maraschino: Italian, cherry-flavored liqueur **Midori**: Japanese melon-flavored liqueur

Noilly Prat: French very dry vermouth

Orgeat: almond-flavored syrup

Pastis: anise-flavored liqueur

Pousse Café: a drink poured in layers to float on top of one another

Quinquina: French, wine-based apéritif, flavored with quinine

Rye whiskey: mainly American and Canadian whiskey, which must be made from a mash containing at least 51 percent rye

Sake: Japanese rice wine

Sambuca: licorice-flavored liqueur

Schnapps: grain-based spirit—available in a range of flavors, including peach and peppermint

Scotch whisky: blends are a mixture of about 40 percent malt and 60 percent grain whisky and are most suitable for cocktails

Slammer: a cocktail mixed by slamming it on the bar

Slivovitz: plum brandy (see Fruit brandy)

Sloe gin: liqueur that is made by steeping sloes in gin

Sour: a spirit-based cocktail containing sugar, and lemon or lime juice

Strega: Italian, herb-flavored liqueur

Sugar syrup: a sweetener (see page 11)

Swedish Punsch: rum-based aromatic drink

Triple sec: colorless, orange-flavored liqueur

Vermouth: wine-based apéritif

Whiskey: spirit distilled from grain or malted barley—the main types are bourbon, rye, Irish, and Scotch

Cocktail List